PRAISE for George Wallace's Poetry

Wake us up, George Wallace! "Beauty as intention" and the music of movement through memory, image, lush lyrical invocation, magnetic mind fields, people and scenes that remain as anchors and engines. Here is velocity, power of forward and backward merged into captivating presence — the shimmering of what endures.

> —Naomi Shihab Nye
> Lanan Fellow, Chancellor of the Academy of American Poets
> Author of *Transfer, You and Yours*, and
> *19 Varieties of Gazelle: Poems of the Middle East*

These pieces stretch the bounds of poetry — rambling passages of language, full of music and changing rhythms, repetition and parallel, dialectic and surreal digression. I admire their ethereal landscape imagery, freely associated, woven around a populist manifesto and haunted by figures of distant romance.

> —Joseph Millar
> NEA, Guggenheim Foundation Fellow
> Author of *Overtime, Blue Rust* and *Kingdom*

George Wallace is a poet who shakes his fist against the shadows, who growls his defiance of the oncoming darkness. There are echoes of Whitman and Ginsberg in his long lines, his cascade of visceral images, his fiery denunciation of the machinery that crushes human beings, his passionate celebration of love and the loss of love, his embrace of life itself in all its mad contradictions. His voice is ecstatic, angry, tender, real and surreal. He is a poet of the city and a poet of the sea, a poet of history and of the moment, a poet of praise for the immigrants who built New York, a poet of prophecy condemning the violence of guns and oil pipelines. There is a powerful energy coursing through these poems, pumping like blood from the heart. 'Who touches this, touches a man,' said Whitman. Yes, indeed.

> —Martín Espada
> Shelley Memorial Award, Guggenheim Foundation Fellow
> Author of *Trouble Ball, The Republic of Poetry*, and
> *Vivas to Those Who Have Failed*

SMASHING ROCK AND STRAIGHT AS RAZORS

NEW POEMS FROM GEORGE WALLACE

BLUE LIGHT PRESS ◈ 1st WORLD PUBLISHING

1st WORLD
PUBLISHING

SAN FRANCISCO ◈ FAIRFIELD ◈ DELHI

WINNER OF THE 2017 BLUE LIGHT BOOK AWARD

SMASHING ROCK AND STRAIGHT AS RAZORS

Copyright ©2017 by George Wallace

1ST WORLD LIBRARY
PO Box 2211
Fairfield, IA 52556
www.1stworldpublishing.com

BLUE LIGHT PRESS
www.bluelightpress.com
Email: bluelightpress@aol.com

BOOK & COVER DESIGN
Melanie Gendron
www.melaniegendron.com

Cover photograph
Wes Candela
wescandelaphotography.com

AUTHOR PHOTOGRAPH
Alexis Rhone Fancher

FIRST EDITION

Library of Congress Control Number: 2017936837

ISBN 9781421837765

"All these human fates and many more of their like ..."

Thomas Mann, *Death In Venice*

ACKNOWLEDGMENT

Grateful acknowledgement to the following publications in which some of these poems have previously appeared: *California Quarterly* (My Grandfather's Song); *Classical Inquiries* (Walking Stride Of Anacreon, Sappho In Her Sweet Repose); *Cloudburst Council Blogspot* (Trail Going); *Cultural Weekly* (Poem In A Coffeepot); *First Literary Review* (Sappho In Winter; You Who Have Been Lost; Nutshell and Flower Bud); *Home Planet News* (Cherry Blossom Tattoo; One-eyed Housecat With A Crooked Tail; In Her Father's House Time Was A Sonata And Everything Was Foretold); *One Day* (Thursday Night Is The Broke Bear Saloon; Night Train Coming; So Many Poets To Give Back To The World; Undressing Moonlight); *Poetsandwriters.com* (The Very Act Of Your Eyes, Shining Like Palestine); *Poets Responding To SB 1070* (Standing Grim In The Harbor And Stubborn On The Prairie); *Poets Speak* (When It's Springtime In America, Fuck You Is In The Air; From The Back Of Your Throat Come Devils And Landlords); *POSTmortem* (Two Clarinets Performing A Punishing Duet); *POSTvote!* (Like A Mess Of Bones In A Jigsaw Puzzle Rock); *Renegade Flowers* (Savage Root, Lifeline of The Heart); *Sensitive Skin* (She Lives In A Little Place Of Boats; Midnight Is Stars And It's Half Past Midnight; I'm A Clocked Out Cowboy And Checkout Time's Eleven); *Speakeasy Magazine* (Cold Like Purloined Ivory Spreads Through His Veins; A City Is Always Disappearing Into The Mist of Itself; War Is Husband To The Man); *South Florida Poetry Review* (Darkness Conveys Awe); *Suffolk Review* (The Language Of Things); *Where the Wurms Play Rugby* (The Highway Died Like James Dean Outside Paso Robles); *Foundling* (From the Back of your Throat; I Am Sorry Diane DiPrima, and Vendor of False Promises).

This collection was made possible in part through a January 2017 residency at Harvard University's Center for Hellenic Studies in Washington D.C.

CONTENTS

WORK

A boy & a girl do as they are told they
walk thru the woods they carry a big
empty basket in their big empty hands
they fill the basket up & they empty it
back out again no it is not peach picking
no not apples — it is spring only spring &
they are young they know what spring
means! My darlings my darlings lie down
in the sweet grass make love in the full-
ness of the season! Green leaves shake &
o the salamanders in their eager laughter!

Freed from the hands of one mad monster
they have fallen into the hands of another

A CITY IS ALWAYS DISAPPEARING INTO THE MIST OF ITSELF

A city is always disappearing into the mist of itself, a gossamer fog of concrete and steel that never stands still and is always tripping over its own feet or rebuilding itself

Out of ashes, out of bones, out of mud and money, and always coming back -- no regrets, leave nothing behind but memory, take nothing with you but the grave

A city takes your heart seriously and hands you back the change, a secret odious flower, sulfuric and idiotic and bright, possessed, acidic, bewitched with the clamor of industry

And the clickclack glamor of mediocre disgrace speaks many languages but not all of them at once and we adorn ourselves and please ourselves with its concoction of petals, grace upon neon grace

The meek and the mild, the rich on high, wearing high heel tottering boots, the high is the charm, it is taller than tall and better than the best and too tall for its own britches

A city wants to look out over its world and admire itself, oh sweet dominion of money, look out, here and here and here, the concrete mix of commerce and sunglasses

Block out the sun, steal the sky, a taxicab always coming, raise up your hand, o warrior, knock me down, rebuild me back all over again, get back up and beg for more, send me your young and your gullible

New faces in the old neighborhood and you can rent this space but not that one, you can't afford to live here anymore, it was cheap once but not no more, this neighborhood's not out of control, man —

It's you, it's you, and all the fuss is the fuss until the fuss is done

Because the city is always disappearing, and when morning comes, there are new cities in place of the old, built for the young, and the cities for the old are the cities to clear out of, to move on from

And they too disappear

DARKNESS CONVEYS AWE

It is night, the sky is marvelous, the city is a place for dislocation, possessions are presents and we rip them open like Christmas, there's rats in the pantry, footsteps on the curb, I love myself in a room full of strangers, a man is a commodity and here's one now, he is wrestling with the elevator door, he must be crazy, but she is madness too, the fragrance of musk is on her clothes

Her hair is a stairwell and the way she comes on to him is a sword in his heart

She was a Lydian goddess once, she plunges and plunges away at his neck, desire is a camel, getting on with things is a desert, nighttime is a taxicab, it is also the traffic itself, everything gets in your way in this town, a man ain't nothing but a dead end

Goddamn it, destination is everything

THIS SCATTERING OF LIGHT IN WHICH
I DISAPPEAR INTO AN IMAGE OF YOU

This scattering of light in which I disappear into your image, the first
anticipation of meeting you, the moment I took your hand and we
turned to walk across a city park, autumn wasn't cold yet, simply to
breathe was magnificent, crisp and cool and the pavement glistened,
a weak light teased the auburn out of your hair, extraordinary light,
natural, swinging along easily

You were always in your element you said, and I was trying to hold
to your gaze while memorizing the movement of your eyes, and the
shape of your mouth, which was a passage from Gabriel Fauré, and
your laughter, which was the ghost of illuminated summer, and your
pensiveness and deliberate conversation — in college it was always
like this, you said, you were the one who didn't roll with the jokes

And picking our way through a crowd of Italian tourists a couple
of gray squirrels sat stupidly in the autumn grass to watch you pass,
and I could read in your stride and in the way you held your body
the careful grace of an educated woman, how to find your way, how
to navigate in an impulsive world, steady, slow, slow, slow, you never
talked down to anybody, not even me, although you knew you could

And your voice was husky with French cigarettes and 20th century
philosophy, and you pronounced my name like it was a perfume, cau-
tiously at first, then boldly, George... George... as a blue and white
wave of pigeons parted in front of us, and I fell hard for you, the full
measure of you, your stride, your resolution, how you pulled us along,
you were taller than me and your accent was perfect

And your shoulders brushed stars from the sky, into the undertow
of autumn, I mean, below the canopy of trees, the leaves of autumn
beginning to fall, on their way to oblivion, and the branches of wild
cherries shimmied in anticipation of your passing, and out on the
street vendors were crying and you wanted a coffee so we sat down at
a cafe, and you shrugged your jacket from your shoulders

What was I expecting, Nirvana?

And your eyes were narrow and you were wearing a white chemise,
a gift from your father, you said, he bought it in Paris, it was his
business to know what was stylish, his taste had always informed
your taste — and yeah, that was an exquisite blouse, so was the
intentional way you leaned forward to kiss me

This is meant to be done slowly, you said. *Intentionally.* Like a promise,
like a disappearance, like a prayer

THIS FISHING VILLAGE WHERE I SPENT MY SUMMER DAYS

I have only to catch the smallest glimpse of the bay through this window, a snapshot of me now between whitewashed walls and roofs of redbaked clay, stucco and glass and mile after mile of drainpipe and gutterwale, and the second story women behind second story sashes with second story lives, friendly with each other but suspicious of this one or that, cutting up carrots and onions and gossiping, gossiping, the secretive orderly good women of the village tending to their children or sitting motionless at the kitchen table with their heads in their hands

And their children, waiting at the front door to be let out, to race to the harbor before the sun goes down, wanting to join in on the raucous, ordinary celebration of the catch — this is the business of the village, gulls overhead and cartwheels and oarlocks rattling, the evening fishing boats are coming in

I have only to separate this curtain in this room and look out sharp between them to catch the marble sea, and the men with their coiled rope and sore shoulders, and the village cats prowling for fish heads, selfishly, the men putting up their gas tanks and lobster pots, they sit on the gunwales gutting fish, a coruscation of light suffuses everything, a collie is barking on the opposite shore

I have only to look out this other way, up into the village, a pathway narrow as the sliver moon that used to cruise among the silver oaks when I was a child, a wooded pathway up to the village church which is the woods where Maria first kissed me

Maria with her thick black hair and her delicate eyelashes, soft as snow, and how she ran away, laughing, and I ran after her — and all the oaks swaying heavenward, to feel my spirit rising, and all that memory flooding back like the tide

This fishing village where I spent my summer days and was entering my teens and there was everything to discover, and so much to be lost, why was I cooped up here with my uncle and my aunt, how I despised their endless dinnertime chatter and childhood slipping through my hands, like fog — what boredom summer heat can throw, what exiles known to man

But still there was Maria's kisses, her straight black hair, her lower lip pulsing, the music of her slim shoulders as she squared herself up against me between the trees, her breath delicate as a rainbow and how she ran and how I ran, and her hand in my hand when we reached the harbor and stopped to catch our breath

We were barefoot and silent among the fishing boats, the mudpools and little shadows were shimmering and salty, strange as jellied eggs in the setting sun, and my feet which had been cut so many times by barnacles and broken glass they didn't even bleed any more

We were two thoughtful children approaching the offices of romance and sex cautiously, with a delicious sense of wonder — what danger, what discovery, what surprise — the sun went down and we picked our way among the crab claws, lobstershells and the amber broken necks of yesterday's beerbottles buried like martyrs in mud and in sand

NUTSHELL AND FLOWER BUD

I have been drinking the wine we made from summer flowers. I fell asleep in sunlight, and now here I am, woke up with a book of poems in my open palms, and the smoky taste of almond blossom in the air.

How long have I been sleeping, why am I outdoors? I touch my lips together, nutshell and flower bud, draw my tongue across my teeth. Sunlight and bright clouds. The sun and the sun, always the sun.

A yellowjacket drowning in a plastic cup. That's my cup, isn't it.

My lips are cold as window plate.

COLD LIKE PURLOINED IVORY SPREADS THROUGH HIS VEINS

He has caught a fever in the jungle and his head is on fire, he is made of straw and is wearing a safari hat, he is crossing a suspension bridge alone on a bicycle, the sun is bright, the East River flows beneath his feet like the ashes of his sister, a plane takes off from LaGuardia, his wife is on it

His wife is a stewardess and she is wearing a cocky hat, he imagines her naked, his joints ache for her, the strangest desires overcome him -- to fly an airplane into the side of a mountain, to fall from the sky, he attempts to lift his head up, no dice

He is attempting to plant tomatoes in his mother's grave, she is young and appears to be wearing his father's clothes, his lips are appleseed, he plants them everywhere, in the sky, in his wife, in a book of short stories by Ernest Hemingway

It is 1958 and these boots were stitched in Buchenwald, his eyelids are golden and heavy, his wife is Swedish and the motion of her hips is delicious, he met her in a bar in Tangiers, her eyes are a martini glass, consciousness escapes him

He sleeps like it is his wedding night, forgetfully, time winds around him like a shroud, it is 1958 the earth is pregnant with the gentle motion of a uterine sea, O I am the Man of Steel, he says, see me on TV! These mortal coils of rope cannot contain him

Life is a pool of water into which a river flows. A man may dip into it with his hands, he says, if he is bold enough, if he is man enough, and to prove this point he brings his palms to his lips and makes a pantomime motion, see, he is drinking

It is 1958, what is that scent in the air, a bug is crawling in his ear canal, night is enormous and pregnant as an insect egg, night has claws and whole philosophies spread their wings to fly

His wife stands over him with a gun, she is made of straw and is absolutely fearless

He tears at his flesh with his fingernails, there are bedbugs in the mattress

What is this fear, cold like purloined ivory spreads through his veins

AN OLD MAN IS STANDING IN THE ICY RAIN

An old man is standing in the icy rain outside
of a coffeeshop on Dyre Avenue in the Bronx
he is an ice age angel in the rain — see how
his hands are folded under his arms like wings —
he is an old man but he casts his eyes over the
world like a young James Dean, shyly, eagerly,
no place to go and no one to go with him
— that's all right — there are traffic lights and
street noises, statues are liquid meth and him?
He's a statue made of ice, he is at one with the
elements, the taste of asphalt is no stranger
to his lips, there's crossing guards, cop cars
cruising, a bus is clearing its throat at the
growling intersection, rainhats and overcoats
and an argument between two women in
the bus shelter, their faces are windows on
the world, the old man is recording everything
he sees, he is the original intelligence, the
little factory of immaculate perception, a
 wise old guru on Dyre Avenue writing
messages to mountaintops (look! he
says, I am an ice angel! ice angel, me!)

Inside the diner a cop at the counter
has his head in his hands, he is praying
for a moment's peace

His pancakes are getting cold

ANOTHER MAN'S RIVER

She is another man's river, she is an iron bit in the wrong man's mouth, she is a horse crossing a river and like it or not her blood is iron and her arms are iron and her arms are stronger than a wolf trap — bridge stock head and jaw — and the marriage vows that bound her are grinding stone

A hoof print in turd. Yeah. A disposition, a means of disposal.

And she's bigger than that, she is a shadow seen through muslin curtains, she is straight adobe and a breeze runs cool across her skin, that's me, I am that breeze and she is a wooden cross with letters in rancher's script, large as sunlight across the adobe wall I can read the name of the one who died

He was large and illiterate, he was husband to her once, and now he is gone, and she cannot grind or cook corn without that man nor wipe his memory away, and now it is me in his place and she is cast iron on an open flame and what do I call her, what do I pray for around here, what do I even call myself

Divining rod, confessional font, certificate of penetration, Man

And she is a riverbed of loving abandonment, and I am a river beneath a river flowing entirely west, west into a basin I will never know, not of my soil, a boulder on a precarious cliff

This digging into, this river rock, this tumbling, tumbling — this sprung trap — this stone tossed into another man's river

SOMETIMES WE STAYED UP HALFWAY INTO THE NIGHT

Sometimes we stayed up halfway into the night and talked about fish, we were obsessed with them — fish like chimneypots, fish with heads like willow trees, croaking fish and flying fish, fish with eyes like stars or hearts like chambers of horrors in a wax museum

Fish like secret poems or love songs written to the rain, fish like xylophones, fish that haul like the furies, that fight so hard they make your back teeth rattle, fish that make your heart go numb, fish that come up out of the water so easy it's like pulling a knife out of a stick of butter

Fish that turn like a windmill in the Spanish wind, that move like young girls, shy at their first dance, or like a cop car on patrol, incessant and slow

We would stay up talking and the talk was always fish. We dissected them or swallowed them whole, like William Blake. Fish. Fish. Ugly as toilets, plain as turnips, fragile as flowers, sad as overturned tractor-trailers. Erogenous fish magic fish or just plain fish, raw and alive.

And one fish like an unexpected jazznote or jigsaw puzzle, racing like a black motorcycle out of a glossy men's magazine and into the world.

TWO CLARINETS PERFORM A PUNISHING DUET

Autumn comes to drink my whiskey and turn the oakleaves red with
death, and I am uneasy with autumn because there's no future in
it, no music, unless you count Richard Strauss' tone poems, which
I do not, unless you look out into the darkness and think about the
complete emptiness of things, which I do sometimes

And autumn is a tin cup that swings from a chain and no one is
there to drink from it, yeah that's raw and a little painful, and the
long blade that goes rusty in the field is also difficult to accept, and
the dark that comes sliding in among us between trees and is a fat
Welsh priest blessing every damn thing he sees as he goes, is painful

And autumn steals everything and walks away, jigging with the
western clouds and making them look stupid, red in the face like
village women with their white petticoats on, Breughel peasants
flinging themselves wild as potato sacks, once more the ride and the
north wind gossiping among the oaks, louder than any damn god

And the last pink rosebuds blushed with cold will be frozen come
morning

And autumn is midnight and violins, and the owl screeching and
the cricket noise, which subsides eventually, and the loon which
dives deep into still black waters — one loon, two loons, go easy
with death — in the hall light, in the porch light, in your daddy's
underwear, in the accumulated dark

Two clarinets perform ingin tune, a punishing duet

SWEET RELEASE IN THE MIST,
MONKS IN BLACK PAJAMAS CHANTING

Sitting at her kitchen window as autumn approaches, winter not
so far behind, brooding over a cup of coffee, I can see the sweep
of rain coming in over her left shoulder, not bitter about it but
there's trouble in her past, full throated revolution about to show its
shimmy, two men in leather jackets smoking cigarettes outside some
Post Restante somewhere and she had to walk past them

It is prayer time again in the Himalayas, she is in an English teashop
with a stranger, wheels are turning in the lingering shrouds, crazy
rivulets of rain are chattering through the downspout like Shinto
Pachinko, like sweet release in the saffron mist and monks in black
pajamas chanting, like Jackson Pollock in the pouring rain, dancing
because the cold wind of Galileo thrills the cosmos

And the monsoon rain has let up at last and all the tin roofs are
littered with jungle leaves and possibly fruit, and troops of monkeys
are climbing out of the trees, lolling about like old men, fat bellied
marauders drunk on Ye Olde Juggernaut and sour judgment, and
the hashish merchant is asleep in his chair, and the moneychanger
reading his horoscope in a month old newspaper

And the Roumanian poet's quoting Sartre per usual and the
suspicious sky's chiming with tambourines and yes, prayer wheels
turning in the sun, lingering, lingering, not wanting to let go of day

How gracelessly rain came down in Salinas, how gray the cattleyard,
her heart was jiving in the heights and she nearly choked in the
gutter in a downtown hotel, her first love was a bowl of hot and
sour and there was always a man at the center of it all, because let's be
honest, the center was shifting in Kansas City her man let her down
and hid his luck, so she just climbed into the nearest truck and sped away

Her memory turns and turns quick, like an old .78 rpm, the cool
bluffs of the Palisades, cliffbirds on Penobscot Bay, nestling in sand,
seagulls in the perennial parking lot waiting for cameras to roll like a
Hollywood Apache in a cowboy movie, and waiting and waiting and
the all-knowing Buddha who lives in the high places and the low
places too, knowing all seasons combine in one, and all flesh

And birds of prey catch small animals, and landscapes collide,
and the fur and fear of small mammals clings to the earth like
ghostshadow of the eagle descending, and she lives in a gilded field
of rust and gold and an incalculable desert of grief and the lonesome
road to Dharamsala

And she got back up, like a pack horse kicking, like anemone flowers
in the eastern valley — like phosphoresence, like henna, like pride —
she got up and she got up

And she burst back open, ripe as the buttons of an Afghan spring

LIKE CONDOR EGGS READY TO HATCH,
LIKE MANIFESTOS WAITING TO BE WRITTEN

I will make love to you in spring, when the world is wet and new, and rivers cascade out of the mountains and stars like suns spiraling out of the spinal cord of creation

In spring, when little heroes race out of classrooms and make faces at the bullies and fascists and there are new gods in this world and dragons are circus animals, and hate is a creature nobody has ever seen before

In spring, when all the world is a revolutionary soldier, and the bearded young men of South America are hatching plots against imperialistas or floating in a Dionysian sea of imaginary blood, like condor eggs ready to hatch, like manifestos waiting to be written

I will make love to you then, like all the blank pages demanding to be filled by a young man who looks up at the sky, licks the stub end of a pencil, and begins his very first poem about nothing in particular

Like a monk who comes out of the cloisters, strips off his frock and wrestles with the other monks, playfully, naked as god in the morning, their bodies fresh as mountain snow, like tigers, like snow leopards

Like lovers making sweet inaudible noises into each other's armpits, they fall to the ground laughing, like a man, like a woman, like an infant reaching out for mother's breasts

So in love we are with the world! So in love!

To touch, to possess, to hold each other, to write our names huge, in big damn democratic letters!

CHERRYBLOSSOM TATTOO

Half made up, all the way crazy, shirt undone and a hairband for a
husband, this bedrock to the lake's slippery as hell, love is a one way
street back in town and it is a slick path down to the water

Spring is no lover but it comes quick and that's how she wants it,
she's got a cherryblossom tattoo on her back, the way she breathes is
rough as bark, sexy, very thick, choked with new leaves and ready for
more

White blossom, there's an old white blossom in her eyes

The lake glows dark and is forgiving and yes, she sits silent and waits,
something's moving down there, something hungry and moving and
wild

A waterbug, a leaf suspended, the quick leap

ONE-EYED HOUSECAT WITH A CROOKED TAIL

I saw a road that climbed halfway to heaven, where it stopped there was a floodgate and a whirlwind and a Dutch windmill and a bolt of lightning

There was a piano and a mirror and a chandelier and miners drinking beer, and bunkbeds and oil rigs and gold

And a Buick with a burnt out clutch

Bedbugs and rattlesnakes and mice in the ranchhouse, and livestock in the holding pen

And a one-eyed housecat with a crooked tail

And behind every rock and tree I saw the government of men, which is a gas powered shovel stuck deep as a needle into the piehole of the world

IN HER FATHER'S HOUSE TIME WAS A SONATA
AND EVERYTHING WAS FORETOLD

What she wanted was to sit in the profound silence of the world, which was greater than the both of them, and greater moreover than that, to sit with him as she sat in her father's house

What she wanted was to let the evening insinuate itself into their lives gradually, and then dance itself out of existence, with its soft radiance, the radiance of a rose, to accept the gestures of time

The way she had been taught, to move easily among the pleasures of her father's house, shadows were enough, in her father's house time was a sonata and everything was foretold

The accumulation of days might have added gracefully to their lives too, if only he would let them

O this man, she wanted to remember each of their days as distinct, each flowing into each other

She wanted to hold his hand and circle him, like a child on her first carousel -- in her imagination life was musical, sharing it was a promenade, she wanted them to fall together into the apogee

To wrap themselves into each other like darkness or the return of day, to suffer with him, to live and die and accept things as they are, until it was all over

But he was not like that, he was like the other men

Remarkable in all the usual ways, always in a hurry even when he was sitting still

What is this fever which possesses them? She would never understand men, so clumsy around her

He was a steampipe fitter, off tune as a calliope, big bold and efficient, his hand in her hands was eager and bright and dumbfounded, useful as a dog or a horse but uncomprehending

He was cautious with his phrases and fearful of the personal, he avoided the invisible realities in which her imagination thrived, the higher sensibilities, like a priest avoids the skin of a leper

You could fit what he knew about women into a clamshell and watch it float out to sea

If a clamshell could float, that is

But they don't

WET AS PAINT, ADRIATIC, DOUSED IN SUNLIGHT

There is no gold in this river, there is only the sunlight passing through, it is oblivion and she craves it, bathes in it, her hair is awash with gold because love is renewable, because her hair is straw, because set against her eyelids which blacken with desire is a European forest, cloaked in unexpected winter light

Because there is a servant waiting in the shadows, because in her left hand is a cushion which does not yield

Her eyes fall on his words, the pupils of her eyes glow like fused glass, her lips speak his words, they are long in the tooth and patrician, they are glorious along the classic lines, tragic, operatic and Italian, the sensibilities of the 16th century escape her, after all she is Northern European, naturally, a woman of her times, in the darkness a string of pearls is draped listlessly beside her, like black sails on the Aegean

Lamplight is a swirl on the page, and her heart is made light

It is her annunciation, now he is Croesus in all his glory, bounty flowing like all the gold of Lydia into the sea and meant for her alone, a beauty meant for no other, this is her river, it will bear him closer to her, into the vernacular of her arms

Lowlandish, Hollander, pale light, gloom — she has waited so long for him, now she is ready for anything, death, decay, the poison of desire, children both living and dead

She thinks she will just drift away, into the river of him, this culmination and buoyancy, feral as musk, dappled, alive, her inner polecat, a fitch of gold, all pelt and petulance

This river that meanders through the body of Anatolia races through her body — a shadow in the antechamber, her temples pulse, all at once her armhairs are awake

It is the wanting, it is the wanting, it has always been the wanting — Sleek beast, wet as paint, Adriatic, doused in sunlight

SAPPHO IN WINTER

She is standing by a willow tree, the top button of her overcoat undone. Her scarf flaps, like a black crow wing, or a calendar in the wind

Solstice morning — earth doesn't know it yet, but she does. Intelligent as a clock, this one. She gazes across the bay, tosses her overcoat at me, walks away

A wet salt wind bathes her cheeks, her breasts, her hair. The same caresses I once gave

HE IS AN ANCHOR IN THE SEA,
SHE IS THE BEARER OF KELP

The sea is deep, the sea is deep, everywhere the morning fog is, is indifferent, it has embraced her since she was a child

There is a blue specter on the horizon, a stupid man rode away, he was here now he is not, she wants more of him, she wants more of anything

Wants her mother to sing to her, wants to hear the one about the cavalier who dives into the sea to recover a golden ring

The cigarette is bitter in her mouth, worse than fog

If things do not change around here she will be forced to take up a trade — spinning, sewing, tatted lace, beat the wash, weave flowers, she who runs her fingers through m'lady's hair — any trade will do

Bored, bored, her finger traces a pair of lips in the window frost, she is muttering to herself, she is an orphan, she has no mother

Thank God for that

This is the originating sea beyond the horizon

She is the bearer of kelp, he is a horse in an open field, which is a sea running nowhere

The sea is muscular, it lifts her up

YOU HAVE SPOKEN TO ME

Yes, you have spoken to me, as in a prophecy
I mean, like a flock of starlings speaks to the
wind, like a wind speaks inevitability to the
oceans to trees, like a grove of trees gives
it all back to the wind, patternweaver, rune-
speaker, poem of the endless air, endlessly
waving, your voice also, sea hillock and wave,
bleating, mad as thistle, yet comforting and
settling into itself, your sweet dampness, the
mysterious vowels of your flight, coordinated
beyond measure, poured like black wine, your
metaphor of going and going and coming back,
a gryphon dancing dark as winter clouds — over
grass and tree, over the mumbling sea of me

NOT LIKE A MESS OF BONES SET
IN JIGSAW PUZZLE ROCK

Not like a mess of bones set in jigsaw puzzle rock for men in khaki
pants to lay claim to, or city fathers to lock up in museums for 4th
graders to press their grubby noses against the glass, witness the past

Not like the movie mosquito froze in amber, or the dinosaur locked
in a crater of bubbling LA creosote

But like a saber tooth tiger trapped in ice, staring down death, fur
and claw intact, full throated bristling prehistoric motherfucker
untamed by wind or by whip, caught in a temporary freeze, preserved
twenty thousand years and this boy's ready to kill and kill again, if
only it can cut itself loose!

This is us, our past, this is ourselves, melting in our own sweet bones,
our crater hearts fill up like melting tundra, our cavernous souls fill
up, and we are ready to spill, it is only a matter of time and there is
no more holding back, the great river of dying flows right through
us, full throated adamant and free

We are about to become glacial icemelt, colliding in a terrible
embrace

UNDRESSING MOONLIGHT

In Vienna I was a fish out of water and suspicious of carriages and horses, being drawn from light to light thru the wet blackness of the Josefplatz, your hand pressed blindly inside mine — your lips were plate glass window pressed to the world, your kisses white wine and fine machinery, your eyes were blue and opaque, and love made sense, it finally made sense

Did you wake some terrible thing up inside me? Yes, something terrible, something wise, some wonderful aspect I needed to remember, like Beethoven, like Mozart, like Brahms or a Tyrolean folksong played on a concertina by a young woman with very small hands and a child clinging to her peasant skirt

And now it is night and the moon follows my train through the mountain pass, and when I wake up I will be in Istanbul, opening a bottle of Old Granddad & pouring one out, in your name, in your name

To the shameless way you have of undressing moonlight

VENDOR OF FALSE PROMISES, THE ESSENTIAL COMMODITY

They pull the cord, they throw you out, the end of all utility, what journeys and circuitry, what electronic impulses, coiled springs and forlorn mattresses, cathode ray, stood out at the corner, torn to ribbons, no longer in service, a life of design and disillusionment

The worst appetites fed, a thousand times worse than bullshit suppressed, suppressed. This for all they channel, this for the faithful servants dying as they go, this for the bullshit, the speeding locomotive, the power we could never contain, clowns, lovers, dishwashers, revolutions of debt

Vendors of false promises, the essential commodity

Dope factotum, jack of all trades, cheap magic to inveigle and to enslave, tubes and transistors to live by, Willie Loman's refrigerator, Bukowski's sorry radio, our meek inheritance, our big payoff, dying the grimacing sullen death of all America

On forepaws, with back legs trailing uselessly, what dignity in death, what entire stupid devotions, channeling dross

What even is this thing called martyrdom, whose Jesus have we here, what unsavory consolations, dumb and broken gifts to ourselves, holy as a wooden spoon, ten thousand dead end Christs dying on forgotten crosses, on every curb and in every dumpster in America

I'M A PUNCHCLOCK COWBOY AND
CHECK OUT TIME'S ELEVEN

Who dressed you in that outfit, throw your shit in the back of the
Toyota and hop in, I'll tell you what it means to be from around
here, needle's on empty and I've been running around in circles all
morning looking for cheap gas, never mind the mutt in the back,
he just can't live in a little box like he's supposed to, guess he's a lot
like me only I keep my big yap shut and don't fart like an outboard
motor, not to mention I keep my nose cleaner than that, sponge in
the bucket if you know what I mean

They used to call this town 'Paradise on the Love Canal' but you
were always ok if you had skin in the game, it was a good old town,
a good old town, even if everybody knew everybody's business and if
you wanted to get your bait wet you better head down to the lake

Pay no attention to that girl leaning on the counter at Piggly Wiggly,
checking out the cowboys and bagging groceries, save that action for
downtown, gets roughneck on the weekend sometimes, haven't been
in awhile but I hear the place is dynamic, most of 'em can't dance,
but a man's a man after a hard week's work and some still got legs

Yeah that's where I work, you can fuck that forklift, I lift those crates
myself

Sure you can come in for a minute, mom's dressed by now and she's
cooking breakfast for the twins, ignore that guy on the couch that's
Uncle Fred he has a persistent cough and a memory of growing up
on a farm, won't stop talking about it -- that old boy will tell you
anything, including just how pretty it can be in the park in July, yeah
hot as jaundice but those trees throw a lot of shade in the afternoon,
and the firehouse does an annual fundraiser and puts up a carousel

You call this coffee, where'd you get this shit it tastes like gravel

No I did not violate no law except seeking to be left alone. Yes I bought this hat at the truck stop and I resent that remark. Yes that one there's Charlie Embers, you've heard about him I suppose. Some strange notions in his head but he's basically solid as a rock quarry, known him since high school, that's a man who knows his football

Let's stop for cigarettes, there's change in the ashtray. Hop out and stretch your legs. I know the springs are shot on this old heap but it's the roads in this town, not me, all these potholes dug by snow plows and eighteen wheelers. There's plenty more to be said about this town but the big thing's this -- keep moving fast forward, that's what counts. At least we've got a stake in this damn country unlike some, and respect the flag

OK yeah I almost forgot, I want to take you down to the lake. You can toss that beercan in the back if you want to. Next to the dog, I'll clean it up later

No of course no great book was ever written about this place, no great picture ever painted. But there's sound barriers to shatter, speed limit zero and in the morning if there are any fences left to mend just give me the coordinates and I'll mend 'em

Yeah I'm a punchclock cowboy, checkout time's eleven

I'm a bombardier in the back seat and you can have your shotgun, buck naked in the blood red sun

STANDING GRIM IN THE HARBOR AND STUBBORN ON THE PRAIRIE

New York or North Dakota, clothed in green, it is always green
beneath the green, copper and gray and wave upon wave, even when
the rain don't fall and the river's fouled, Lakota green the sweep of
snow, Lenape green the Hudson flow, bullboat paddle, earthlodge,
dome, buffalo rock, green, green and green against the government,
green against the tear gas, green against rubber bullets, sound
cannons and concussion grenades

And grim in the harbor and stubborn on the prairie, o unwed
mother of orphans, give shelter to the dispossessed, put food in
the mouth of the hungry, and in the eyes of the ones who will be
oppressed no longer, put courage to flip the government's fucking
humvees into the Little Missouri, and in the hearts of children who
watch from the window, courage to send their asses packing with
slingshots and arrows

You stand rock solid in the green waves of prairie grass, a different
sort of beacon, and I get that, a lantern is a lantern, lifting itself up
and daring to disturb the universe of money, men, and ingenuity,
and soldiers with guns to back them up — it's always the same story,
Lady Liberty in the slopewash plains and yes your eyes are two black
suns in the silverblue sky, staring down money and oil, oil and money

And money is money and footprints of greed are blueprints drawn
on sacred land, and what are these pipelines to us, pouring oil on
water is an insult to water, we only get one planet, it is enchanting
even in darkness, and justice is a woman, and she's blind like my
sister the rancher, married to a copper-colored goat, a filthy man,
they have a spread in Montana and connections in high places, and
when we sleep down by the river we will have to keep our eyes open
for them

And bat wings are angels overhead, and I do not mean to be strange about it, just sensible to be invisible, invisible there is nothing to fear, this all belongs to us, what can I say, the scent of horse flesh, the taste of pueblo dust and saddle leather, the sound of you breathing here beside me tonight, riding all night to where the sweetwater flows

This is Lakota land, no one should be stupid enough to disturb it

LESS GUNS = MORE LOVE

"I dreamed I saw each one of us armed with weapons of love"

Don't talk to me about guns talk to me about deadly force — can I put this killing machine into my own two bloody hands or into the hands of others

I know foolish men I know evil men and ordinary guys I know men who make mistakes or are all thumbs can I put this deadly force into the hands of them

Men who are easy to anger or quick to judge I know men who go blind with rage men who lose their heads at the drop of a hat in the heat of the moment or when dinner's late

Men who are sore losers or insecure immature drunks weaklings momma's boys and revenge seeking nuts can I put deadly force into the hands of them

The paranoid the childish the suicidal and the impulse junkies let them express themselves with a killing machine instead of a box of crayons or fists on the floor

Let them have their tantrum of tears let them pour bullets over their heads or hurl them at each other like bowls of milk like Rice Crispies

But keep their butterfingers off of shotguns handguns and semi-automatic six gun shooting pistols

Don't tell me about guns tell me about Andy Lee of Woodstock NY, only sixteen, captain of the HS football team, shot in the chest on a cold winter day in January

Tell me about a nation where a man can kill a man but cannot marry him — not that I want to do either but some men might —

Can I let them have the one but not the other — good men bad medicine men holy men and angry men crooks and librarians?

What makes one man sing the blues what makes another man pull a trigger?

O give us this day our daily sulk give us our grievances for crying out loud give us this day our daily wounds to lick and pick at, our scores to settle

But do not give us killing power
For we will use it

WAR IS HUSBAND TO THE MAN

Setting cold meat on his dinner plate how to explain this thing to his wife especially in front of the children, the neighbors are listening at the window — there's madness in the basement, it's war at eight —

A firefighter flips his mashed potatoes off his plate a cop parachutes into bed — how to explain the tracer bullets the blue concussions the comets and blackouts — how to explain the stars in heaven

No they aren't so bad just so they stay in heaven where they belong

He says her name like a prayer — o apple pie o nest of vipers o shrapnel wings — now I lay me down to sleep I pray the lord my soul to foxhole pajamas — zip me up send me home

No I am not an American flag in your fucking lapel mister I am a house on fire — soldier boy o my little with this ring I thee wed — no letting go no turning back — war's a smokescreen, war is husband to the man

Honey here comes the stuttering bride
She's got a bayonet for a tongue

POEM IN A COFFEEPOT

Life was good
it was finally good
there was God in the popcorn
poems in the coffeepot
there was sandlots
and crackerjacks
and picklejars and
pitchers of beer
There was tenements
and bosses and
Coney Island holidays
and the immigrants came
and the immigrants came
in their immigrant pants
and their immigrant dresses
and they built New York
out of glass and steel
in their own immigrant image
Olive oil and eggplant
prayer shawl
candelabra
chicken fat and wine
and they kept on coming
with their accents and their
operatics and their strange
music halls and melodramas
and stubborn political sciences —
Eastern Europeans, Southern Europeans,
Polish, Russian, Italians,
Jews, Greeks and Germans —
And they kept their big traps shut
when they were forced to but
they stuck to their guns

and they took the dirty jobs in the
dirty factories and the lights went out
on Saturday night at quarter past ten
and bedposts shook and radiators
rattled like an elevated railway and
late night jazz — and the stubborn lights
of New York City glittering like a knife
thrust deep into the heart of heaven
— and the immigrants of NYC
wrestled with each other
in the dead of night

For love, for loss
For consolation
For unreasonable
Unstoppable
Unnatural
Hope

OUR FOOD IN YOUR HANDS

How can a man walk thru a supermarket anywhere in America
without feeling the imprint of your hands on everything he touches
— hands strung in the dawn of cinch bug nematodes smell of dung
— plastic buckets bandanas & shorthandled tools — hands which dream
of beanfields straw beds & barbed wire — cornsilk & buttermilk —
the watery music which leaps like fish out of blue mestizo night like
your family's laughter & into day

You migrate thru South Carolina like drift of fog you harvest
tomatoes in Florida you migrate thru Delaware Maryland
Connecticut & Maine you harvest potatoes apples soybeans peas
beets — beets spinach & beets — you tend to broilers heifers hens &
sows — you harvest wild rice you pick avocados & grapes you plant
white tufts of cloud into the hair of your children like seeds in heaven

O lettuce! O bold Salinas valley! — O crates of California!

Plums apricots Oregon cherries in plastic bags — in low country &
on the high mountaintops cucumbers string beans brussel sprouts
walnuts peaches & almonds — oysters in their shells — broadcast
spreaders sprinkler pipes & burlap sacks — how can any man
woman or child in Colorado Alabama Arkansas Missouri Louisiana
or Illinois — any man woman or child in Cochise County Arizona
or New York City

Ever walk through an American supermarket without feeling the
power of your steady eyes — balancing every crop & planted field
in America against the remaining hours of day — your back your
neck your feet your shoulders & especially your hands — whole
families of hands — tired cut bruised bug-bit hard with work —
unwitnessed underpaid ripped off & oh yes ready to take being
kicked out

Because you come back, don't you, you always come back — you
burn thru mist like the border sun, which migrates thru every
supermarket in America

I AM SORRY DIANE DIPRIMA

I am sorry Diane DiPrima there was no
revolution, we cleaned things up just
about enough to carry on, we forgot
your necessary guns and Buddha,
the revolution of the body and heart
was no match for clean sheets and
prosperity, we brought down the man
and filled the lakes back up with rainbow
trout, we unpolluted the sky, closed the
factories and gentrified the Lower East Side,
hell I think it was a Rockefeller uncovered
the Sawmill River (have you seen the Bronx
River Parkway sparkling in the autumn sun),
we filled our gas tanks and bank accounts and
ran off to Cancun, into the mouths of our children
we poured laughter fireworks poetry and college
degrees, we forgot about filling our bathtubs up
with your grandpa's Marxism and coal, the life-
preserving waters of Sacco & Vanzetti went
down the drain, escaped us — we put aside
your revolutionary letters and let our cup
runneth over with patriotism and football,
and craft beer, yeah we let the old sins
back in — success for the many, fuck-all for
the few — until the few became the many
again and now it's fuck-all for everyone
except the fatcats and their plastic wives in
golfcarts, country clubs and private towers,
and all the cleanup we done's about to get
undone — reach for the sky, the privileged few
are on high protected by their trolls and goons
and the rest of us hanging around the streets to fool
and to fuel, it's ten PM, 3 drunks crossing Church Street

pull on a young girl's hijab and shout Trump Trump
Trump — and the blood in the eyes of the people,
and the anger in their mouths, is for each other,
not for the oppressors — just the way they like it —
and where is the precious seed of your revolution
now, Diane DiPrima, when we really need it

FROM THE BACK OF YOUR THROAT COME DEVILS AND LANDLORDS

& what is this strange ointment, this dubious trill of a Queens canary, this handwrit promissory note, uncollectible, bust up the string quartet why don't you

Make a fool of old shovelfoot, kneel down on the throat of the slide trombone, climb on top you twitterheaded tanktop eraser, you piping hot lie machine — melt down microphone

Yes yes I have heard the deep bop of your new flambeau, it fools everyone, must've learned that in a TV script or straight from Putin —

And yes, you strapped-on uptown tight-lipped motherfucker, tossing matches into the gas tank of America to see what's what

Inflammatory racketeer dressed in scorchers, nomad seductor

From the back of your throat come devils and landlords, dressed in the latest demon demoiselles, this sinuous accountancy, a factorial zero in the mink

Nubile, erect, cantering puttyfinger, pussy grabbing nobody jacked up like a star

O eminent domain discount narcissus

O heavenly trinket, self-declared, the root of my pain, I feel you in my spine

O let down your hair, unglamorous warrior

WHEN IT'S SPRINGTIME IN AMERICA,
FUCK YOU IS IN THE AIR

Trump Tower New York City the pleasant little solitaire the bold
lonely penthouse gestures all the sexy stock options and stupid
surprises on every platform and corner a proposition for you
dear everywhere you look like a turnstile of love you look like the
crosshairs of money

A revolving door of indices and economic indicators what ails you,
my girl my girl

You are one lucky sonofabitch living on the top floor in the
meatwheel of America New York New York uneasy oasis of
jerkweed Coca Cola and look at your name in every windowpane a
newminted coin in your mouth a sensational woman to poke

Who got the big chromium smile you! Who got the smart ridiculous
rollsuit you! Idiot, not to mention in a big damn hurry

O mister pocketpants with your poppa's money to throw around,
your hookers and slaves your stink of knock-off French perfume,
you snap-on cheap ass pay your bills, pussy tree — rev it up screw it
down piss it out on cobblestones

The rainbow shines for you o shaky braky nastyman. Meet me by the
unlisted telephone number. With rage all right. With deals all right.

Huge deals.
Bum deals.

Choke it back thrust it out let's get it done.

CARRY YOU HOME FROM THE FAIR

You are a rowboat of wild horses and tomatoes
we are sailing home across a surreal fishbowl
this is summer, stupid yeah,

Is that a mixed metaphor? So what — you won
a goldfish and held my hand, we bent the rules
we can ride the back roads

Grammar is good romance is better real love is
possible and it's better to swim with the cannibals
than lie down with the clams

Who's drowning? Not us! Every moment should be
beautiful like this, o bliss o cotton candy o carousel
kisses! It's your birthday

Let me take you home to our goldfish bowl — I am
the bubbleman I live at the bottom of the tank —
and you to me are better

Than Shakespeare in a car full of roses

I will carry you home carefully,
i will carry you home

SHE LIVES IN A LITTLE PLACE OF BOATS

Like a housecat put out after dinner
like a sailing man with noisy pockets
like one of Neptune's nasty daughters
or bicycle chains or mopping water
she lives in a little place of boats
with a stranger's baby for a bride
with a pail of hooks for a heart
with a cloud of seaweed for eyes

O crazy seachains! o net of lies!
    O fish guts caught in cobblestones!

This is no sea shanty, and no she is not
a lie. O wharf rat bigger than a porkpie
hat! She lives in a place of no dreams,
where the lungs of fishing boats fill up,
in the slapping prison of night, they fill
up with yawping silt and slinky brine —

She walks the streets with the moon
    and throws down moon beams all night long.

MIDNIGHT IS STARS AND IT'S HALF PAST MIDNIGHT

Midnight is stars and it's half past midnight, and a man may sing, a man may sing, a jug of wine is the full measure of joy, all this talk about the beauty of the world and universal suffering, heaven is in the air and always with us, air still hot but it feels like 50, and we're sitting by a sputtering fire, so what! Two shy Buddhas content with rain in our joints and a set of wrenches you can depend on, two traveling gentlemen our backs to the dark and our eyes on each other, and the flame leaps up, higher than missionary walls

And no we are not much more than a couple of bums in leather jackets, but with temporary work and our shoulders hunched up we are something else tonight, bullshitting kings, two beautiful imaginary lords of money, philosophy, women or nothing at all, two burning stars amid all the usual west coast mythologies, a band of coyotes in the grapes, a nightfall of calamities and rust in the railyard, rust in the brakes, rust in the kitchen and the hotel pipes, and friendship is trust and what can two strangers do, hold secret with hope and true to each other

The rattlesnakes still bite, the old remedies apply, rust is the linkage of a thousand other stubborn mechanical difficulties and a jug of wine is a roadmap through stars

As for rust it can wait til morning, just mix a little salt into lemon juice and set it out in the sun while we sleep til noon

By the creek I mean, where the yellow grass sings, and the crickets gone slumbering in the lavendar shadows

TRAIL GOING

Here we are at the doorway to the heart, take
my hand, what tempos we will discover, what
companionships, take my hand or go it alone
I am with you, my heart races with yours, the
sweet bronzing of your skin is my skin too . . .

My eyes blink away the same cobwebs and tears
as yours

OLD WALT, GROOVY AS A SPIDER

Old Walt, groovy as a spider, subtle as spun cable, your perfect balance under new stars, your promises and opportunities, groovy in the sense that the old rising sun is new and strong, subtle too, in the sense that spanning the Delaware, criss-crossing continents, is subtle

Ironworking man admirable as a continent, Walt from your high roost and perch of iron, no drifting tranquil river for you, strong hands for the split rock instead, tugboats churning, daylight spitting back with sweat and lunatic dust, strong bridges named after you and hopefully the universe is generous

And the grinning stupidity of commerce and crowds is not stupid at all, but groovy and perfect and subtle, conducive to what is right and holy

I give you yourself, Walt! In overalls, in torn pants, with hard hat and poor workingman boots, your bridge of iron, your sledgehammer fist singing in sunbright May — your limits breached, your harnesses and your husbandry — your dams and thrumming cities and open land

I give you limitless waters, Walt Whitman! The spectacle of new bridges! Your admirable traffic of men and machines in sweet natural dawn!

THIS HAMMER IS VICTORY, THIS CHAIN
THE DEFENDER OF THE CAPITALIST SYSTEM

I pull out my pocket comb I run it through my hair, the smoke
screen of civilizations, I am a convict and I am on parole, I am huge
material categories of sexy, this hammer is generosity, this chain is
liberty, this pulley is criminal, this handtruck unsympathetic, and life
falls down dead on the weeping floor

My hips are cannibalistic, my eyes look away, look away, and I walk
the delicate walk of a tipsy child — these joints agitate for you, these
arms sing the kind of rhythm and blues you have never known —
yes an indelicate pain is in the orchard, raw as cotton, the moment
falls away from your shoulders like sunlight from a flower, my kisses
sweet as falling rain

I would offer you anything right about now to become a part of you,
I am a place on earth between heaven and hell, Dionysus is blues in
a bottle, place your hand on my knee, your palm to my beard, the
aberrant throne of supplication, your lips are wings of gypsy moths,
my palms are pilgrims against the darkness

Your breast hurts my eyes, my eyes are a pilgrimage of biblical
proportions

This scripture is tractor dust, I can open you up now to any page and
see the signs, this book of numbers which is a prophecy, my lips at
the marble quarry, I am smashing rock and straight as razors

We own nothing except what the man has given to us to own, and
what he wants he takes, it is the natural order of things — waterfalls
belong to heaven and a man returns to his moon

What we have we have, until we are completely undone, what we
sow we spill, harvest and plow back under

We will rise up again in new fields
like floodwaters rise, like junebugs
in flickering light we will rise again

This action, these lips, rising —
against you, against your lips,

Rising — your lips against mine

SAVAGE ROOT, LIFELINE OF THE HEART

Meadow flower, flower which is naïve idiotic & beautiful all at the
same time, meadow with its flesh pulled back, savage root, lifeline of
the heart

Un abbraccio che mi faccia sentire, I am a meadow flower, haunted by
the sun, whereas some people want to be the sun

Sun which is a reckless lover & burns holes in captivity, sun which
churns up seeds like butter in the sour belly of planet earth

Sun which busts fields open with its fists, pries apart the earth with
its fingers, takes what it wants & leaves

Sun which abandons earth to the half twilight

Shitfaced speechless dumb & alone sun

Make love to strangers, make love to no one at all

ANEMONE

Strange new flower, a woman, a man, androgyny torn from a patch
of earth, and shadow, where morning sunlight cannot reach it, face
petal breastplate sword, a monotype, what it means to be this, the
meaning of this, lobed, parted or undivided, petals on a strong thick
stem

What is this song this ballet this grief

Windflower sketched in white chalk, shy lover stealing across raven
run, flowering in the stiff sawgrass, unholy places born, reborn, hush,
hush, strange new spilling over, hush, opening in the wild wood,
an herb, a poison, a fleeting star, plant made flesh, woman, man,
filament, blood, goddess, goddess, goddess

Godless the flower and the blood-flecked boar

Tiny secret of the unopened petal, Adonis locked in dew, embryo of
the fleshy fruit, eaten and eaten by mouth and by hand, this woman-
wood, this man-filament, this anticipation, stigma, stylus, and of
course the ovule, overwhelming blossom of a woman-child, forest
giving birth to itself, strange hybrid insinuation

Strange new flower that repeats itself, insists on itself, is androgynous
and youthful and beautifully born

Flower of deception and death and rebirth, terrible provenance,
strange new stealth in the landscape

Vindicate us, Venus' delicate grief

BLACK CROWS FORAGE YOUR HEART
LIKE DOROTHY IN A POPPY FIELD

Farmer's blade, forester's axe, on account of you, millions die, you open your mouth, you walk out into the sun, a cold wind slams the oak door shut behind you.

You order a beer, you pour a cold one out. Golden extinctions in every glass, in your shallow breathing whole prairies where hooved creatures used to run, light a match, see the ruin.

Lift a book, read the words. The truth is Pravda, generations lie dead in your hand, whole forests fallen.

Your bones are threshed wheat, your lips are mangled fruit, in every loaf of bread, cactus flowers shaking. In every slice of pie, seed upon seed crushed underfoot. Your stomach is filled with untold slaughter.

Black crows forage your heart like Dorothy in a field of poppies. A grindstone turn cartwheels across your tongue, every step you take is a killing field. Your voice is a wind farm, your pretty poetry ghosts of trilobites.

Fossils, all of it, and stolen.

Your dreams are a harvest of owls, the cries of the unprotected inhabit your brain. Grasslands fuel your computations.

Make no excuses, the fabric of your coat is woven with blood from a thousand laborers' hands. Onions bounce past your door like circus clowns, doing tricks for you.

The truth of the matter is beyond endurance.
There is a twig in your heart. Eat of it.

THE HIGHWAY DIED LIKE JAMES DEAN OUTSIDE PASO ROBLES

True story we were alive back then we were lovers in the tall grass outside Paso Robles where California meets the golden sky, there was cattle grazing and I got the pictures to prove it, we were legal back then that's what the draft card said, we were perishable young hipsters of the 60s, wet behind the ears, back then I mean her hair was black, her skin porcelain and we hitch-hiked across America, left Bronxville with 38 bucks between us that didn't matter, I had never fallen for a girl like that and we were on the trance road to our own true selves

It was the western trail to smoky paradise and we were holy brave and new and the miles passed like a poem, we crossed the big river in Iowa, caught the long ride out of Davenport, 6 a.m.

The big rigs were flying and she sat between me and a trucker named Mel, from Laramie to Salt Lake City we listened to West Texas junkie tunes on the tape deck and slept in ditches, and when we woke up there was prairie dogs and the horizon was diamonds and the western sky turned Hunke gold and there was prisms of light in the shot glass, and the waitress was kind to us at Jack's Café, I guess the radioactive soup of the wild American West hadn't gotten to her yet, *Why you're just a couple of kids* she said *fancy that!*

On the sixth day out she left me sleeping in the middle of the night and never said goodbye

THURSDAY NIGHT IS THE BROKE BEAR SALOON

Just another night in a rust belt town but it's our town and it's the
Broke Bear Saloon, not much on the jukebox except the usual doom,
so what, enjoy yourself, Thursday night is an American tradition, any
night really, Henry, try to slow down and enjoy the scenery, let's take
this thing one shot at a time and see what happens

Yeah I got money, who cares how I come by it — the fuck, okay see
that woman over there at the bar, got it from her, yeah she's got a
friend, looks a little strange but that one's got a mouth like Cape
Canaveral, it was her that says you take this money and haul your
shit over to your friend, have some fun, just save a little of your sweet
self for me

Gotta respect a woman like that, anyhow here's blood in your eye
and mud in the gutter — I'll be right there honey! Pour your ass out
on the dance floor, I'm right behind you

Say Henry, wasn't it just the shit coming over tonight, fog thick as
gravy, dark by five? I know yeah of course it's late November, the
snowbirds have all flown south, what's that leave us? Take what you
can, throw it in the pan with cooking butter

Damn this place stinks like a dead raccoon

No, don't scratch that thing you'll make it bleed

No Henry, that toilet hasn't flushed in a week

RAIN BEAT DOWN ON ROUTE 22, SPECTACULAR!

Paterson New Jersey was never very lucky for me, especially back in
'86 but sometimes even a boy from here gets lucky & if he doesn't
so what life doesn't come with guarantees, around here you stay at
home or you take your chances & yes it was like that in the '80s an
unholy decade of suicides & shoddy analysis unless you were one of
those on Wall Street

Which no I was obviously not, some assholes went hardcore punk
but what was I going to do, some of the others had tight pants and
hair out to here, that was out of the question so it was simple — sit
at home & watch the NJ Nets go 24-58 or hang out at the bar & get
stupid with beer and blow with a cat named Old Man Winter

I don't even know why we called him that, he was the same age as us
but his hair was white, played jazz trumpet in the high school band,
a real time yeti, I sat behind him in the trombone section, he was
usually lit up like Xmas, sitting there by himself at the bar eating his
fist like it was prime rib — a monarch among men — & normal re-
ally, considering the time & the place, fucking New Jersey, of course
all the wrong drugs

And here it was New Year's Eve and on this special day neither of
us had anything to discuss or intelligent on our minds, the deep of
winter was about to dump all over the world, the simple horrible
equation of shitty weather which is the Northeast in January. and
of course the joyous banging head-on collision of life which was
Ronald Reagan's America, at that particular time it was all very
phony & sadistic, brass balls & free underwear, some serious bullshit
was unfolding, the fake generation was upon us

When just then from across the room in she comes waltzing, the
first honest ray of sunshine I'd seen in a month, she loped in like
a Stopwatch Goldilocks, walked straight up to us like we were the

Three Bears & she was Slippery When Wet & she just had to pop a
question and land it square on us — neither Old Man Winter nor I
knew what to say so we put on our Sunday School best, smiled & let
her do the talking

She wished, she said, to know how to get back to the I-95 she and
her amigo had gotten themselves turned around on the turnpike &
which exit was it to the Meadowlands, Secaucus, because some band
was playing there, they were from her home town & she had to see
them or she would just die, moreover she had this friend, if we cared
to show them the way well we could come along for the ride

New Year's Eve, rain beat down on Route 22, spectacular!

It was inevitable you could just smell what was going to happen
next — the whole damn world was about to explode, someone
somewhere was going to tear down some fucking wall in Russia in
China in Germany somewhere & why not & why not us?

So we got in the car & we drove
Old Man Winter was not immune

ON WHEELER HILL

There's been a drought around here for a long time, the promised
rain didn't come today, nothing but a strung out old crow who stole a
strawberry right out of Eddie's hand, but stars here dazzle too, living
off the grid

Some say things that disappear appear again, such as my reading
glasses but not the shoes I wore; and Saturday morning is a ghost
mist swallowing up everything, and Wheeler Hill is a thin sun
creeping in like a yellow cat after a rough night out with the coyotes

And there were beaver in the swimming hole once but someone
poached them out, according to the man who came to confess and
he bust out crying

In the afternoon when we gathered under the windy tent a couple of
long legged neighbor boys showed up, standing on top of a wagon
full of split wood, and Craig read poems as the boys pushed back
their wide brim hats and the dray horses stood patient as "got-all-day,"
and Craig didn't lose his stride as a couple of us helped chuck the
wood into a crazy pile in the tall grass and goldenrod

And I counted 60 under the tent, poets I mean, and not enough
chairs, they came from everywhere including Virginia, one guy
propped up an uncut log and sat on that, and the wind blew strong
and the tentpoles shaking

And when the poetry was done the sun went down and the firepit
sparks in the firepit commenced to flying, and the Czarnecki boys
played guitar under the tent until one of the grand kids got crying,
and a lot of the others hung around the fire til 2 and there was no
more bourbon

And it was all good, all good, and in the morning I found my glasses but not my shoes, so I took a drive on the ridge road, shoeless and with morning breaking, just me and a murder of crows and a line of small deer with white tails and leaping manners

Three shy punctuation marks high tailing it across the cut corn and Quaker hay

LOOSE STRIFE

All great art escapes boundaries — and you are a kind of great art to
me — like a rosebud unfolding from pink coral — like a painting of
a dance which becomes the dance itself — like a game of giant steps,
like city kids chasing each other across the jazzy schoolyard pave-
ment

A dark samba plays under weeping maples, released into the world
by young men in a city park, a dark samba takes love by the hand, to
places love's wings have never gone — like your love for me which
escapes all reason and escapes itself — like my love for you, which
covers

Entire meadows, entire meadows, occupies the wetlands along the
edge of the great road headed north, filling up with an unexpected
symmetry of white butterflies

It is August, white butterflies are everywhere, there is trouble and
beauty in the world, and the graceful yellow sun in our windshield
passing — your love for me, my love for you, and a dark samba
which has let loose on the world —

Many white butterflies, and these tall stalks of purple flowers,
loosestrife

THERE IS A KIND OF BLISS & SADNESS TOO

There is a kind of bliss, & sadness too — a mother's
day poem transmitted thru raindrops and cities

Rain, which holds onto everything at once & knows
nothing & knows the difference — & windowpanes

Which understand nothing, nothing at all, beyond
the raw futility of trying to hold certain things in

& certain things out.

THE POETRY OF RESISTANCE

In this dream I am chasing along a riverbank & maybe you have
had this dream too — I am tugging at a kite string & the kite tugs
back & we have an understanding this kite & me, we have this
conversation

Like Woody Guthrie in the cottonwoods, talking to the trees
Like Woody Guthrie in the cottonwoods, talking to the wind

This kite is writing the poetry of resistance in the big blue
chalkboard of the world

This kite is writing the poetry of emptiness in the big blue
chalkboard of the world

This kite is writing folk songs & I am singing more power to
you, kite! more power to you!

& more power to all the regular folk standing on riverbanks
everywhere, wondering which way

The world is pulling them, and should they stay & fight, or
should they up & go

In this dream, I mean, in this dream

Like a kite string in the wind
Like an astronomical river

NEAR TO THE SKY

I could not imagine how
you trained your words to
go around in circles like that —
like circus elephants — so
I went to the circus, to study
you. The popcorn was stale.
Clowns? Predictable. Honestly,
I didn't like seeing horses
being treated like that.
But O the acrobats!
How they made my heart
rise — so terribly near to the sky
I almost forgot how you lied to me

SO MANY POETS TO GIVE BACK TO THE WORLD

I sat at the table I drank with the others, in the gray of the eternal gray we sang our songs and let him pass, what else was there to do, forsythia blossoms in the world and then fades and there are so many poets to give the world back to, and one less among us to wrestle with

The god of guitars must be happy he got what he was after

To walk out into the world with April like Eliot said is a kind of death and the cold fate of it, the fuel and fact of it, the world made new, the world made goldendew and here comes this jet stream of death, one less among us, time revs up careless and cruel

And om to that and om to that

And the yellow flowers, and the greening leaves, and the wine and laughter, I just don't know if I can take another day of it, knowing that forsythia wait for spring to blow and that poets notice, and that the wind is cold and mist sings with birds, and one more of us is gone

NIGHT TRAIN COMING

Night train coming, seagulls are circling the dark skies of your city,
there is news from the front and the news ain't good, broke tooth,
spear through the chest, smelt iron heated beyond all recognition

I am the melting pot and I bear terrible news, war is closing in on us,
if you touch my skin troops will come pouring out, my guts are grief,
my legs are a deluge, I am molten lead and I am dangerous

This rag in my hand was a schoolboy once, this broken spine is a book
of Latin verbs -- how can I conjugate this, what are the declensions,
my teacher is hate and I am a bridge across the Monangahela

I come from nowhere and I am going nowhere

THE LANGUAGE OF THINGS

We are proud of our sweet selves we are mutual magic we inhabit this
place there is music in everything, we speak the language of birds —
we own nothing and so what! Nothing owns us — we owe we touch
we communicate and what's the difference if the light in the sky
which dropped us down and left us here is gracelessly dying

We are parents of our own image and our bodies are our children we
know it we use it we eat it up drink it down we build and build and
still we make admire and ignore, we invest we mean we tough it out
and laugh everything off

We labor in the dark and wake up emptyhanded in the cold morning
of our own miscreation, our children are curious about that so we
allow them to examine us for cracks and blemishes

A boychild peers from a storm drain he is a raccoon in a black mask

A girlchild gathers up in the palm of a hand she is a broken flask
and froze in concrete

Our children are cutlery, man! I mean I hear them rattling in
cupboards and drawers and falling off countertops like raindrops like
forked lightning, they are earthquake and a molten choir

You can hear them through apartment walls

You can see them thru windows, blue halo of streetlight

Wreathed in black magic rodeo dust, songbirds in the mist and the
rabid snarl of taxicabs

A WANDERER'S SONG

Wander crazy as a cloud, not quite lonely, be an itinerant cloud
that's all right, be like rain, a curious cat a circus a parade, a new age
Houdini or Kerouac wearing slipknots, a jug of wine for the ladies
and whiskey for the lads, half learned jokes and a couple of poorly
concealed aces

Every town is a low cottage with doves in the attic and one too many
daffodils, no kitchenpots left to slap no money left on the table, and
who wants a table when morning's come, no taxes no trials no axes
to be sharpened, no knives to grind, no battles to be joined in on

And the sun is a woman who keeps on moving and nobody's figured
that out yet, and the trees are children who stay in one place and
require rainfall and watering, and it makes a man cry to sit under the
same sad rooftop and sing his song and die slowly

Because if you don't keep moving life is lonely and tragic too, even
when it is beautiful besides, and you have to be curious about that
and keep on traveling and never wonder why, there are mysteries
around the corner, there are possibilities and visions

And questions that cannot be asked properly or erased or wiped away

And every place is no place at all or someone else's place already, so
why fight it and what can be done about that — scent the prize take
your chance get asked to leave — and wander, somewhat lonely and
certainly crazy

Because stillness is okay for bedrock and gurus, but not for men, not
for men, and graves dug deep are not for the living, and a cloud is a
cloud and loneliness is better than nothing

THE VERY ACT OF YOUR EYES, SHINING LIKE PALESTINE

Thistle goes to seed and so do men,
and no I am not religious and neither
am I dying, not just yet, I am night,
night is steady, night is a map with
no stars, how many thousand years
have come and gone and I am all of
them and only a few, there is no guide
to go by, and that's okay, the wisdom
of centuries is an old-fashioned notion,
the lines in the palm of our hands are
message enough

This weak signal, this alien intelligence
which rules our lives, Dante wouldn't
like that, what is wanted is a fixed point
in the night, something steady we can go
by, something reliable as perfect lovers,
breathing together, internalizing each other,
or this small cloud which crosses your face
when you are sad, the ghost of a Jesuit priest
slipping through a courtyard, like doubt
or the wind, like Lorca or a grain of sand
from some apostolic desert captured in
a jar, like you lighting a cigarette, or me
lighting a cigarette for you

Like time itself, lighting itself up, because
time is immortal and doubles back on itself,
and wind blows smoke into your face like
the sulphur of Troy, and night is the skin of
St Sebastian pierced by a thousand arrows —

as full of arrows as a sea urchin — and yes you
are absentminded and your love is accidental,
we were all young once and loved, though not
in equal portions of pain

Share your mouth with me like the limpid moon —
press your mouth to heaven — say whatever you
wish, speak into the abyss, that's why it is there —
with your voice which is satin, with your lips
which are freed slaves and the color of brushed
gold, with your eyes which are Andalucian, your
small voice singing like an orange grove in rain and
on a night like this I can imagine you in a previous
life, a pony in a corral, your blood racing, hooves
trampling everything in your path — cactus, rock
and clod of earth

The very act of your body, reincarnation, a Lydian harbor;
The very act of your voice, sacrificial among Greek sails

The very act of your eyes, shining like Palestine

MIRAGE

Sometimes when the sun comes up you can see them walking in quavering light. Dance and whirl 'til there's no dance left, only the light of the sun. Sometimes the sky is so blue, so blue!

The clouds move through this land with an infinite patience, a slow grace. Borderland, like a Mexican waltz, like a mirage. This I think is how the desert answers prayer.

A man I know rode two days thru this desert, praying; he followed a flock of birds like a map, the earth was level and dry, for two days he prayed to Yaya-uhca, god of the black maize, and he rode.

His eyes gleamed with a slow fever growing, his throat rattled in the lingua franca of the desert; on the third day he could ride no further and he laid down to die.

In his own shadow, I mean. He laid down to die in his own shadow, right here on the border. With his money and his mirage, with his phony papers. With his dreams of America, he laid down to die.

But the healing waters began to flow.

THIS IS WHAT MAKES ME SADDEST, LEAVES FALLING FROM A SWEETGUM TREE

I think of you often in your blue negligee, awake tonight on the outskirts of town and you with the upstairs light still burning - this is what makes me saddest, leaves falling from a sweetgum tree, gravity pulling the old house down, brick by brick until the last brick falls, chainlink fence shaking wet with cold, your eyes like a collie

Your eyes like a coffin with no roof, an open book on your chest and your heavy breathing, while the road and me and the interstate, a head-on collision, going crazy across the hedgerow and into a field where the fat cows graze, creekbed for a pillow, offering myself to the wind, to emptiness

And I wish I could have been content to lie with you and die pleasantly, but borders challenge us to cross them, transgression is our one reliable law, that's narrative fiction 101, a fundamental rule of action in novels or romance, and o what sweet madness the body reveals beyond the blue practicum of order, beyond the recipe meant to subdue us

So we tear down the convenience store of our days, so we join the road which keeps ticking come storm or come stew, and now life is steady and sure, and now life is a commuter train run smack off the railroad track — and yes, this sacred spot, and yes this glorious field

And yes, these weeds and bottles and this memory of you

BEAUTY IS INTENTIONAL, BEAUTY IS AN ACT OF THE IMAGINATION

Beauty is intentional, beauty is an act of the imagination, beauty is resistance and she crosses the cobblestones like a deck of well-shuffled cards, her hands are free, in her blouse her breasts are swinging — they are a pair of doves, perfectly suspended, confirmed by the gods, her eyes look out in either direction, they are the blueblack handiwork of Olympians, two tourist gondolas soar over ski slopes, up and up and over Italian wine country, a gaggle of holiday goers crowds the windowpane, what Dionysian celebration, what debauchery and anticipation

And o what sweet regrets, all this precipitous going, year after year they climb and climb and never look back, they never fail, what can match this balanced panorama, nature and human enterprise join hands, see the spectacle before it's gone, how could anyone miss this chance, glorious cable cars and what's to stop them, their dizzy elevation, their defiance of time

And she is shy, in her glance gravity itself ceases to exist, no future past or destination, only the rocking, easy miracle, only the cloud motion and eagerness

In the elemental sun, to know, to know,
And, equally in return, to be known

SPLIT ROCK SUTRA

December 21, 7:17, dawn rises over Pelham Bay, fifty five hundred
seventy seven miles away bombs explode, there is bloodshed in
Aleppo but there is also a ceasefire and the ceasefire is holding, and
47 children trapped in an orphanage in Eastern Aleppo are being
evacuated, some in critical condition, many with life threatening
injuries or suffering from dehydration

47 orphans boarding UN buses today, children in winter clothes
carrying small backpacks or playing with kittens, and Trump
doesn't want them, and Europe doesn't want them, an increasingly
globalized world is frightened, voters have had their say, the Patriotic
Europeans Against the Islamization of the Occident, the Alt-Right,
Breitbart, they have all had their say

And thousands of refugees are getting on buses in bitter winter
weather, and all the war dust and all the dead, and all the concrete
flying ('the aircraft began to strike as if there's no such thing as
a cease-fire or evacuation of civilians') but what can we do about
it, asks Trump, 'we don't know who they are, we don't know who
they are or where they're from,' says the Donald, 'they have no
documentation, folks, they might be ISIS!'

("My house collapsed," says a woman in a blood stained hijab on the
news report, she is beating her chest, her lips are busted wide open
with grief, "all my children are dead")

("My students are mourning," says a law professor in Delhi, India,
"mourning for the people of Aleppo")

20,000 refugees, 47 orphans, buses from the Shiite villages, buses
from Eastern Aleppo, and the solstice sun rises over Pelham Bay
(Dutch soldiers overran this land, burning Lenape villages)

287 Congressmen against them, 31 U.S. governors against them, any number of Syrian refugees may be too many for the Donald (Lenape soldiers overran this land, burning European villages)

And Anne Hutchinson died, and so did all her children (except Susannah, eight years old, who hid behind a split rock and watched as her family was massacred)

And Chief Wampage found Susannah hiding behind Split Rock, and he rescued her and raised her as his own (he even changed his name to Anne Hutchinson, 'thus being honored by using the name of his most famous victim')

But we cannot let this happen people, we cannot let this happen, they might want to join the ranks of those who hate our institutions and want to overthrow them

And the fighting is not over, it is not over, large parts of the country are controlled by armed insurgent and radical groups, and other parts of the country by the regime

And the war is advancing and the refugees are streaming out

And 47 orphans are getting on board UN buses in Eastern Aleppo, and they cannot come here

KNOWLEDGE IS A PRISON, SHE IS A RIOT
IN CELLBLOCK 49

This is not Memphis, she is not Cleopatra, the Roanoke river is not blue lightning and she has not been drinking from a whiskey bottle - she is a white cloud, her face is a mirror and when the wind parts the curtains it lets the white clouds out, and she is one of them, one of the clouds, what's wrong with that - and the sound outside her window is not blue jays quarreling, and field mice are not nesting in the hedge, and a motorcycle is not revving up the gravel drive, bringing him home, bringing him home, and what was she supposed to be doing anyway, she is doing what she is doing, something practical and to be expected

This accidental thing called love, she smiles to herself, and her smile is a condescension to smile, and she arranges her hair with her hands because she knows how to do that, and daylight streaks through the room like the image of her mother in a photograph, imperious, particular, talented, young to a fault, and in addition to being herself she is a portrait of her mother, everyone's always said that and she knows it's true, everything she knows has always been true and natural and right there in front of her, present and true, it all culminates in her, is her, and anyone who would say otherwise is a liar

Anyhow who could say no in this little room, she can hear everything that's coming right here inside it

She has auburn hair and it cascades, it cascades, and her skin is white and delicate, *like porcelain*, she says, *my skin is like porcelain*, she has thought about that a lot but she's not going to think about it all day, and this is her entire vocabulary, it is a language of remembering, and she is still as a housecat walking through the room, the ghost of a housecat who used to live in this room, her room on the solitary third floor, her father's father built this old place, it faces west and

the afternoon is quiet, and this is her identity, her sanctuary and
where is that comb, where is that damned comb

The idiom and the accent of her hair will have to wait, she looks in
the mirror, see how her hair composes itself

Knowledge is a prison, she is a riot in cellblock 49, her forehead
is a ridgetop, you could ride along with her forever, like a troop of
cavalry, chivalrous, with her eyes which are colorless though they are
bursting with light! the color of black walnut, the color of rebellion,
the color of Jack Daniels — and no this is not her hand, and no this
is not her hair, and no these are not furrows in the corn, this is not
dust over wheatfields or a motorcycle ripping up the gravel

And no this is not the ghost of her grandfather, crawling out of a
Fredericksburg trench

Or lost in a forest somewhere in the Ardennes following the sun
with his eyes, the winter sun looking westward and home

SONG OF MY GRANDFATHER

An old man sits by
the sea and loves
too much and not
enough, he sits by
the sea counting the
waves, and his heart
pumps salt water and
cries like the wind as
it passes across the
face of the world, and
his blood is made from
salt and brine and
little sea fishes and
the waves come in
groups of twelve and
pass him by — and
he embraces them,
he embraces them,
one by one, in their
terrible going, with
his eyes, with his
arms, with his
wretched pain
and imagination,
knowing each
will escape him
but that there are
always new waves
coming — and
the sea spray
and the sand
and all that
nothingness,

knowing in
his deep
blue sea
heart

there is a thirteenth wave.

WHEN I AM OLD AND IN LOVE

When I am old and in love, and my shadow is drunk with it and
I have nothing left to hide but rare mountain herbs to clothe you,
when I am indelicate and have no secrets, unchaste, a mad species, a
naked old fool with empty hands

When I am a man who no longer knows his own name, a man who
trembles in terrible spring because voices in imaginary mountains are
calling

When I am bone to bone with death but on my way back, and pour
myself into your heart like glass at midnight, and pour myself out,
when I am a ruin to everything I touch except you, you who admire
me like a prize mountain goat, prancing old idiot with eyes swirling
like a swan that swirls thru cosmos

And when I am made new, and up to no good, and you are a goddess
and want my frail human heart

When I am sacrifice itself and my shadow runs right through me,
drawn from fire like a sword and plunged into ice, forge of souls
seeking transformation and new identity, when recklessness is my
kiss and an oracle, when the sun runs up into the sky and I run from
light to light and my heart is a cult of you, a basket of deplorable
mysteries, my words burnt on a pyre

Here, priestess to the dark dance, we shall attend these mysteries,
you and I, around this altar, wearing a garland of bridal flowers

Leaves, grasses, flowers —
branches and a noose

THE WALKING STRIDE OF ANACREON, SAPPHO IN HER SWEET REPOSE

To know time, know where it comes from, where it has gone, to
measure moment against moment, star gazing, love making, the
blood of heaven, the seed of gods carried in the wind, the sundial,
measure and not measure, open up the throat and let the universe in,
to sing and be silent, to be the maiden in the mirror, the young man
at the lyre

To remain the same, this cycle of song which is no song, this
unbroken mystery, counting the hours — girl to woman to girl, lyre
to hip, plectrum in hand, garlands of bindweed strung and worn in
the hair, strew your bed with purple flowers, grow and stay, walk in
the radiance of the sun

To pause and to move as if you are dancing, as if you are motionless,
to move as if you are permanent, the fixture and motion of time,
inside the sacral passageway, outside the harmonies and spheres, rock
on rain on rain on rock

To be sacral with sunlight, which is day and the absence of day, to
know where time has gone, where it has come from, to experience
the convulsion of time as it turns in on itself — like a grey flower

Asphodel, melodic, contemplative, eternally moving, motionless as a
funerary urn

To know the contexts and the conventions, the human
imponderables and designs, to walk like Anacreon, sing like Sappho
in her sweet repose, call time by its given name, which is horos, horos

To be the sun, and not the sun —
To be the sundial, which is also the rain

WINDOW OF PERPETUAL LIGHT

What shall I say, what shall I do, tell you what I am, how I got here,
stand on a platform and touch a star, rip a phonebook in half and
pull it back together again, sing you a song of endless beginnings,
argonaut of the celestial vault

It does not signify and does not signify, I am neither master of
time nor slave, subject to old age like the rest, death and decay
and resurrection await me, this is what i wanted to say, what flows
through you flows through me,

The funnel of a man is no measure of anything at all, and that is
perfect and fine, I am resilient to nothing and everything, except for
love and you, and you are proof itself, destination, you shine on me as
sunlight shines on the shy face of a leaf,

A diamond, the open mouth of a tunnel, a sweet sutra of emptiness,
you dance like Morpheus on my lips and yes you are a river, breathe
out and out, breathe out and out and in, the ocean is huge, life is
permeable and the taste of salt,

The tide is nothing, shadow of darkness, nothing, a river that is calm
runs beyond itself and into itself, a river that runs too swift and stops
too quickly soon runs out, here is the map of the known world, tear
it up, be with me tonight

Boundless as Anaximander's window of perpetual light

PATIENCE IS A STONE THAT KEEPS ON TURNING

Out of shovel and pick, out of soil and bone, I choose you, we do what we will, we are to this place what we are to each other, flesh, bone, what water is to earth when it creeps through hearts and what I say is this, the wind is silent the earth is silent and we are waiting

And what water is to the sky when it falls from the sky and the people look up and are blind to heaven, we are that to each other, we dig for a thing we cannot fathom, we dig through the dark and worship what we do not understand, love til death makes us stop —

What is the air compared to this, what is this parting, this corruption that elevates us as it drags us down, all of us flesh and the offering of flesh, carve it in stone, make monuments of it, dig its likeness out of mountains and rich veins, fashion vessels out of clay, pour fresh water into sand

Patience is a stone that keeps on turning, and eternity is a pebble buried too deep to be found but we keep on digging, and I put aside decay and I choose you —

Here is a woman dressed in a gown, her lips are the color of pomegranate; here is a man lying naked on the ground, his scars are deep, his skin is the color of buttercups and his eyes are stone, and there is no god but the god who lives in root and bone,

And there is no horse but the horse that won the race and fell on his knees to the ground — it is skeleton now — and flesh is loam, the teeth of heroes gleaming in the dark, jaws, muscles, bronze and bone of heroes who fought or ran, all returned to soil

And the nymph who gave her name to this place is gone

YOU WHO HAVE BEEN LOST

You who have been lost,
you who have been hated,
you who have been loved,
loathed or glorified, what-
ever your circumstances,
come with me this morning,
into the mist, into the pine,
 be at peace with yourself,
the old veil is parted

It is a new sweet morning,
be at peace with yourself.

ABOUT THE AUTHOR

"If you want to know what America feels like in your mouth," writes the *Huffington Post, "read George Wallace's poems out loud."* George Wallace is Writer in Residence at the Walt Whitman Birthplace (2011-present), first poet laureate of Suffolk County NY, and author of 30 chapbooks of poetry. A seminal figure on the New York City poetry performance scene, Wallace maintains an active international schedule of workshops, lecture presentations and poetry readings. An adjunct professor of English at Pace University and Westchester Community College, he is editor of *Poetrybay, Walt's Corner,* and co-editor of *Great Weather For Media* and *Long Island Quarterly.* In 2015 he was named laureate of the International Beat Poetry Festival.

www.ingramcontent.com/pod-product-compliance
Lightning Source LLC
Chambersburg PA
CBHW032023090426
42741CB00006B/713